Deepwater

Carole Wilkinson

HORWITZ
MARTIN

HORWITZ
MARTIN

Horwitz Martin Education
A Division of Horwitz
  Publications Pty Ltd
55 Chandos St
St Leonards NSW 2065
Australia

Horwitz Martin Education
Unit 15, Cressex Enterprise Centre
Lincoln Road
High Wycombe, Bucks HP12 3RL
United Kingdom

a black dog book
Designed by Josie Semmler
Illustrations by Graeme Wright pp. i, iii, iv, 9, 11, 14, 16, 19, 23, 27,
30, 32, 34, 39, 49, 51, 52, 59, 61, 65, 67, 72, 74, 80, 84, 87, 88.
Illustrations by Peter Mather pp. 15, 82.
Cover illustration: Mini Goss.
The editor would like to thank the following for permission to
reproduce images: Aqualung, pp. 43, 44, 46, 48, 50, 53, 54, 55, 56;
Healsville Sanctuary, p. 4; Heritage Victoria, pp. 71, 77; The Photo
Library p. 7; Seal Rock Victoria Australia Pty Ltd, p. 26. Other
images are from the editor's, author's and designer's collections or
are in the public domain. Every effort has been made to contact
original sources, where known, for permissions. If an infringement
has inadvertently occurred, the editor wishes to apologise.
The publisher and editor would like to thank Garry Chapman and
Vicki Hazell, the educational consultants on the series.

National Library of Australia
Cataloguing information
Wilkinson, Carole, 1950– .
  Deepwater.

  ISBN 0 7253 1659 4.

  I. Title. (Series: Phenomena).

A823.3

Printed and bound in Australia by
Sands Print Group Ltd
2 3 4 5
00 01 02

Contents

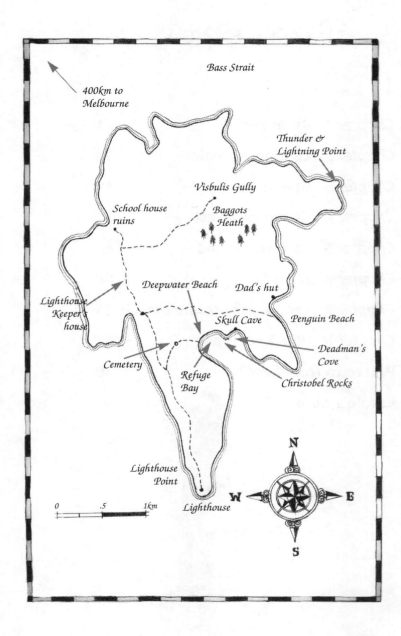

Bass Strait

400km to
Melbourne

Thunder &
Lightning Point

Visbulis Gully

School house
ruins

Baggots
Heath

Lighthouse
Keeper's
house

Deepwater Beach

Dad's hut

Skull Cave

Penguin Beach

Deadman's
Cove

Cemetery

Refuge
Bay

Christobel Rocks

Lighthouse
Point

0   .5   1km

Lighthouse

N

W   E

S

chapter 1
All at sea

THE WIND STUNG Vincent's face taking his breath away. It was so cold he thought his nostrils would freeze. He could imagine his father saying, "This is the freshest air you'll ever breathe. Straight from Antarctica. Wonderful isn't it?" He'd said that about fifty times since they'd arrived on Sandwich Island. Vincent didn't think there was anything wonderful about the constant wind.

He kept walking through the tea-tree shrub. The ground dropped away and the grey sea suddenly stretched out below him. At the bottom of the cliff there was a thin strand of yellow. A beach. Bazza sat and panted.

"Come on, Baz. You can make it a bit further."

Vincent followed the path down the steep slope until it dwindled away in a dune of sand. The wind disappeared. Despite the cold weather, Vincent took off his shoes and socks and walked along the beach. The sand felt good between his toes.

"This must be the only beach on the whole island."

It wasn't a big beach, not much more than 100 metres long and curved like a crescent moon. There had been a storm the night before and the beach was strewn with lengths of giant kelp, pieces of driftwood and rubbish. Usually the wind blew from the west as Sandwich Island was right in the line of the Roaring Forties. Sometimes it blew up from the south, straight from Antarctica. Vincent had never known it to blow from the east before.

At each end of the beach there was a pile of big rocks, which gave natural protection. Between the rocks the beach formed a sheltered cove. The sea was calm now. The waves tumbled onto the sand and bubbled up the beach. Vincent quite liked the idea of his own private beach. Not that he wanted to swim. But it

Giant kelp is a type of seaweed. It is one of the fastest growing plants in the world. It can grow up to 50 cm per day and can reach lengths of 30 metres. Kelp is rich in vitamins and minerals and is eaten in some parts of the world.

was good to have a place where there was no wind.

Vincent turned and looked at his footprints in the sand. He felt like an explorer, the first person to set foot on these sands. He wasn't of course. There was an old, tumbledown boat shed which was locked. He peered in through the dirty window. There was no boat, but there was some old rescue equipment and a few fishing floats. Vincent picked up a piece of driftwood and threw it for Bazza. Bazza flopped on his back and wriggled in the sand.

"You're supposed to bring it back."

Bazza smiled his doggy smile and didn't move.

Vincent walked up the beach and sat down on one of the rocks. He was determined to get used to the sea, to shake off his stupid childish fear that it was out to get him. Vincent had never liked the sea much. It was big and wet and dangerous. As a small child he'd cried whenever he went to the beach. The way the sea rushed up the sand had scared him. He thought it was after him. His parents had made him learn to swim, but that hadn't helped.

The Roaring Forties are parts of the ocean in the Southern Hemisphere between 40° and 50° latitude south. They are famous for gale-force winds.

3

Then they'd moved inland to Broken Hill for a few years, while Dad was making documentaries about echidnas and blind moles. Vincent had never grown out of his fear of the sea.

Vincent held his breath as he watched the next wave surge up around his rock and then slowly suck away again.

"It's okay," he said to himself. "There's nothing to be afraid of."

For a few moments the sand around the rocks was visible before the next wave came in. Something was glittering in the sand. Vincent waited for the water to go back so that he could have another look. There it was again. He counted how long there was between waves. It was about twenty-five seconds. When the next wave ebbed out, Vincent was ready. He jumped down and dug his fingers into the coarse wet sand. It was a coin, a gold coin.

He'd need both hands to clamber back up the rocks, so he put the coin in his jeans pocket. Then he thought he could see another glinting coin in the sand. Vincent bent down. He was knocked off his feet. The incoming wave bashed him

Echidnas have spines for protection and long noses and claws so that they can dig for their favourite foods—ants and termites.

against the rock. He cried out with pain and got a mouthful of sea water. He had been counting in his head. He'd only got to nineteen.

Why had he ever thought that he could trust the sea? He tried to get his footing in the sand, but as the wave washed back out, the undertow was so strong it pulled his feet from under him. He struggled in the water, trying to swim against the pull of the sea, but his efforts were useless. He was washed out of his depth.

Sand is formed by the waves breaking and grinding larger pebbles and pieces of rocks into much smaller particles.

The next wave picked him up and hurled him back towards the shore. He grabbed at the rock as he was slammed against it, but it was slippery with seaweed and he couldn't get a grip. The panic rose in him as he fought for a hold. He swallowed more sea water and it burned his throat. I'm going to die, he thought as he was washed out to sea again. His arms and legs hurt they were so cold. He couldn't fight against the sea, it was too strong.

Then he heard Bazza and he could see the old dog at the edge of the water on

---

undertow: *the current which flows back to sea after a wave has crashed on the beach.*

---

the other side of the rocks. Vincent had to get clear of the rocks. He struck out sideways in the few brief seconds of stillness as the wave changed direction. He swam for all he was worth. The wave picked him up, but he kept on swimming parallel to the wave. Each stroke moved him no more than a few centimetres, but by the time the wave reached the shore he was clear of the rocks and was washed up on the beach. The sea hadn't finished with him though. The sucking water pulled him back out again.

He remembered Dad unsuccessfully trying to teach him to boogie board when he was about seven. He had to ride the wave in. He got ready for the next wave and started swimming just before the crest got to him. The wave carried him back to the beach. His arms felt too heavy to lift but he made them move. With his last strength, he pulled himself through the water until his flailing arms were digging into the sand.

Then he scrambled to his knees and crawled up the beach away from the

> **boogie board:** *a small foam surfboard used for body surfing.*

sucking sea. Bazza came and licked his face. The dog's warm tongue made Vincent realise how freezing he was. His legs were stiff with cold, but weak, like they were made of jelly, at the same time. He knew he had to get warm.

Vincent felt so miserable and sore that tears were running down his face. It seemed ten times further back to the house than it had on the way down.

He'd only been gone a couple of hours and luckily the fire was still glowing. He put on more logs and stripped off his cold wet clothes. Then he wrapped himself in a blanket.

Penguins are birds that are only found in the Southern Hemisphere. The penguins on Sandwich Island are called Little Penguins. They are the smallest penguins in the world—about 33 cm tall.

When he woke, he thought he was back in the city. He knew he wasn't at home. Where was he? Over at Albie's place? No. It was too quiet. Then he saw Bazza stretched out on the rug and it all came rushing back to him. He was on Sandwich Island. Just him, his father and 2000 penguins on this speck of an island in Bass Strait. The mainland was only seventy-five kilometres away. On a clear day you were supposed to be able to see it. So far there hadn't been a clear day.

He got up and rang his mother, even

though he was only supposed to make calls after 6 o'clock or on weekends. When he heard her cheerful voice, a terrible wave of homesickness hit him.

"I want to come home, Mum. I won't do anything else wrong. I promise. I've been working really hard at my schoolwork. You've got to let me come home."

There was a beep on the other end of the line. It was just the answering machine. His mother wasn't home.

He thought of all the days and months stretching ahead of him. He couldn't do it. Tears rolled down his face. He curled up in a ball on the rug by the fire. Bazza came and lay next to him. He put his arms around the smelly old dog and drifted off to sleep again.

Vincent woke to find his father standing over him. The fire had burned down again and Vincent was shivering inside the blanket. He didn't feel good.

"I got knocked over by a wave." Vincent was expecting a lecture about carelessness and lack of responsibility but it didn't come. He must have fallen asleep again because the next thing he knew, the fire was roaring and Dad was picking him up and putting him in a hot bath. It felt wonderful. He was too stiff to get out of the bath by himself and his dad had to almost lift him out. Vincent caught a glimpse of himself in the bathroom mirror. He had enormous bruises on his arms and legs and his face was badly cut and grazed. Dad helped him into a track suit.

"Better not mention this to your mother, Vincent," his father said as he heated up some tinned soup. "We don't want to worry her."

chapter 2
Lighthouse Point

D AD BROUGHT VINCENT breakfast in bed. He'd found the walkie-talkies that Mum had given them so they could stay in contact when Dad was at Penguin Beach. They'd carried them for the first week, but never used them. Once the batteries went flat they'd forgotten about them. Dad had recharged the batteries.

"I'm okay, Dad. I can get up today." It had taken Vincent two days to get over the cold he'd caught in the water.

"You don't have to. Only get up if you're sure you've recovered."

His father finished his coffee, put on his waterproof jacket and left for Penguin Beach. He'd done that every day, seven days a week for the two months they'd been on Sandwich Island. That's what he'd be doing every day for the next three months: going off to sit in a hut and film the penguins. Vincent watched the stooped figure of his father shuffle off down the path muttering to himself, his untidy grey hair blowing about in the wind. Vincent had friends whose grandfathers were younger than his dad.

It was Mum's idea that he come with his father to Sandwich Island. She had freaked out completely when he was expelled from school. She felt sure he was on the way to a life of crime. He'd told her that it had been a one-off mistake. It was stupid of him to go along with the others, he admitted that. He knew it was dangerous, but he didn't want the others to think he was scared. He wouldn't do anything like that again.

He'd been angry with his mother the whole time he'd been on the island. Albie's mum had been furious too, but she hadn't sent Albie away.

The phone rang. It was his mother.

"I'm sorry I missed your call. I've been away for a few days," she said. "Are you okay? You sounded pretty upset."

Penguins swim instead of fly. They eat small fish such as pilchards and anchovies and can travel up to 50 km each day searching for food.

"No, I'm not okay. I've been sick. I'm lonely and bored. What do you expect? No-one enjoys punishment."

"It's not punishment, Vincent," his mother said. He heard the catch in her voice and felt glad and guilty all at the same time. "It'll be a good experience for you on the island. And it's a chance for you and your father to get a bit closer."

So far that hadn't happened. Dad was just as wrapped up in his work and as silent as ever.

"It'll also give you time to work out what you want to do."

Vincent wasn't even thirteen yet, how was he supposed to know what he wanted to do for the rest of his life?

"Not the rest of your life," his mum had said when she announced he was going. "You need to make some decisions and consider your attitude to school. I'll miss you, Vincent. But I think this is the right thing to do."

His parents had always worried about him. Every kid went through phases, but Vincent's phases were short. They were convinced he was never going to settle on anything. He'd been into roller-blading for a couple of months and

got sick of falling over. He'd tried out for
the basketball team, but never went to
training. He'd saved up his pocket money
to buy a second-hand guitar, but found
that learning chords was far too boring.

The only time Vincent had ever had a
firm idea about what he wanted to be
when he grew up was when he was
about eight. He'd decided he wanted to
be a detective. This was when all his
friends wanted to be astronauts or long-
distance truck drivers. Vincent had put a
sign on his bedroom door that said,
"Vincent S. Visbulis, Undercover
Detective" and had gone around looking
for people to investigate.

He spent weeks investigating why Mr
Zollo across the road drove off at 5.30
every morning only to come back again
just before 7 a.m. Vincent was convinced
he had something to do with gangsters.
After weeks of intensive investigation, he
discovered that Mr Zollo owned a
laundromat and went to open it every
morning. His parents had hated his
detective games. They thought he'd
picked up the idea from watching TV
shows round at Albie's. That was
probably true. Vincent's parents refused

to have a television in the house. He'd had to beg his mother to let him bring video games to Sandwich Island.

His parents were both into nature. They didn't think any experience was worthwhile unless it involved sleeping outdoors somewhere very hot, very cold or very wet. Dad spent months in uncomfortable places filming. Vincent's mother was a lecturer in botany and went on field trips every year to study tiny plants that no-one else even noticed.

They wanted Vincent to be like them, devoted to conservation and wildlife. When he was younger, they'd never bought him the toys that he asked for at Christmas. He always got the sort of things they wanted him to like: an ant farm, an aquarium, a set of wildlife encyclopaedias. The ants and the fish died and he hardly even looked at the encyclopaedias.

Vincent built a fire and made himself a toasted cheese sandwich. It wasn't until he was sitting in front of a blazing fire,

---

botany: *the study of plants.*

14

sipping a hot chocolate, and sharing his sandwich with Bazza, that he remembered what had caused his latest troubles. The coin. His jeans were in the laundry trough, still damp and crusted with salt.

He felt in the pocket and found the coin. It was big and so shiny it could have been brand new. Vincent was pretty sure it was gold. On one side was a picture of a man in a robe carrying a small ship in one hand. On the other was a shield and a cross. It had some words in a language he didn't recognise. There was no date, but it was old, you could tell that by the way the picture was stamped off-centre.

The writing on the coin said "Zelator Fidei Usque Ad Mortem" which is Latin for Defender of the faith until death.

"I wonder if it's from a sunken ship?" But Bazza was more interested in the remains of Vincent's sandwich than an old coin.

The day he'd got dumped by the wave had been the first time Vincent had done any real exploring on the island. The weather had been terrible the whole time they'd been there. Much of the time the wind was so strong that it was difficult to stand up. Vincent looked out of the window. It was raining but the wind wasn't too bad. He'd played all the video games till he knew them backwards. And if he played Revenge of the Vampire Zombies one more time, he'd go crazy. There were wallabies in the garden eating the lettuces that the old lighthouse keeper had grown and which had now gone to seed. If the wallabies could put up with the weather, so could he.

"What do you reckon, Bazza? Shall we go out for a walk?"

Bazza was an old blue heeler kelpie cross. The last lighthouse keeper had left him behind. Bazza came with the house. He spent most of each day asleep in a grimy corduroy beanbag near the fire. He had a strange way of getting into the squishy chair. He would stand along side it and sort of fall sideways onto it, then wriggle his bum until he'd made a nest in the middle. Once comfortable, he wouldn't move.

Vincent had vowed he wouldn't start talking to the dog. Albie had a dog. Albie's family talked to the dog more than they did to each other. They had a special high-pitched voice they used when they were talking to it. After eight weeks on the island, Vincent was now having long conversations with Bazza.

The red-necked wallaby lives on islands in Bass Strait. It has grey to reddish fur with a black muzzle, black paws, black-tipped ears, and a dark brown stripe between its eyes.

Vincent dangled a big iron key in front of the dog. "Let's go and take a look at the lighthouse."

Bazza wagged his tail slowly and rather unenthusiastically.

Vincent contacted his father with the walkie-talkie.

"I'm feeling all right now. I'm going out for a walk."

"Are you sure you're up to it?"

"I'll be fine, Dad. I'll take it easy."

"Call me when you get back."

Vincent put on his coat and set off towards the lighthouse. He was a bit stiff because of the cuts and bruises, but he took it slowly and his legs gradually got moving again.

"We might eventually get a permanent sideways lean, like those trees," Vincent said. Bazza walked alongside him in the rain. He had his tail between his legs.

"I didn't say you had to come with me."

If trees grow in a place where there is constant strong wind, they will grow bent away from the wind.

chapter 3
Gravestones

Australian mainland

BASS STRAIT

Tasmania

THE ISLAND was one of the small islands of Bass Strait, only about two kilometres from east to west and barely four kilometres from the top to the end of the point at the south. It was a lump of rock with steep cliffs leading down to rocky shorelines that were constantly pounded by crashing waves. The only vegetation was low and scrubby.

The lighthouse was out on the point, a good three kilometres from the house. There was a path through the bush but it hadn't been used much since the lighthouse was switched off. The path climbed up and down with the hills and the valleys of the island. By the time the lighthouse came into view, the rain had stopped. Vincent was thirsty and sweating.

"Why didn't you remind me to bring a water bottle?" asked Vincent as he watched Bazza lap rainwater from a puddle.

The lighthouse was tall, probably twenty metres high with a red, iron railing around a little balcony about three-quarters of the way up. On top was a glassed in section where the light was. It was just how a lighthouse was supposed to look, but it wasn't used any more.

The light had been turned off in 1995 and replaced by a small navigational beacon on the edge of the cliff. The new light was less than a metre high and was powered by two solar panels. It was automatic. It didn't need a team of people tending it day and night. Vincent's father checked the beacon once a month and cleaned the solar panels. That was all that was required to keep it in full-time operation.

The last keeper had stayed on for a couple of years after the light was turned off, but then he'd had to go back to the

Bass Strait: *the channel of ocean between mainland Australia and the island of Tasmania.*

mainland because of his health. Vincent wondered who would check the beacon after they were gone.

The lighthouse was built close to the edge of the cliff. It was a long way down to the sea, more than 200 metres. Even though it was a pretty calm day, the waves were crashing onto the rocks below with a tremendous force.

In 1822, a French physicist, Augustin Fresnel, invented a lens that was made up of rings of glass that concentrate the light so that it could be seen from a long way away.

Vincent fitted the key into the lock and opened the door. He climbed up the iron stairs. At the bottom the walls were one and a half metres of solid stone, towards the top they were still nearly a metre thick. There were eighty steps. When the spiral stairs ended, another straight set of steps, almost as steep as a ladder, led up into the area where the actual light was.

The light globe was still there and was surprisingly small, but it was surrounded by complicated circular lenses, which must have magnified the light. There was a wooden swivel chair, some old telegraph equipment, a tattered map of the island and binoculars hanging on a hook. The clouds were starting to break-up. There was a 360-degree view from up there. Vincent could see a container ship far out to sea. There were two other islands not far away. From the map he worked out they were Seal Island and Windswept Rocks.

He felt safe in the lighthouse. The sea didn't seem so threatening from behind the glass. Bazza found a patch of sunlight to lie in. There were a couple of cardboard boxes on the desk and one on the floor, half-packed.

The boxes were mainly full of journals, where all the lighthouse keepers had written daily reports of their duties. They should have been sent somewhere for storage. The old keeper probably forgot.

Vincent flicked through the pages. They were pretty boring. They started in 1846, the year that the lighthouse was built, and went right up to 1995.

The early journals were full of uninteresting details about what time the light was lit, how much oil was used and whether the flame was burning well. There were also daily weather reports that sounded depressingly familiar.

Dull cloudy weather. Steady showers. Foggy and damp. Strong winds.

The electric light globe used in a lighthouse is around 1000 watts. That's a hundred times stronger than this one, that we use in our homes.

He put the journals back in their box.

Vincent decided to walk back a different way. The path he chose snaked through tea-tree shrub. In some places the tea-tree on either side of the path met overhead and made a tunnel. Vincent had to bend down to get through.

He tripped over a piece of rotting wood and almost fell on his face. It wasn't a branch or a root that he'd fallen over, but a fence post with a length of rusty wire through it. He followed the wire to what looked like the remains of a gate. Vincent parted the prickly bushes and forced his way through and up a slope.

Lighthouses are round because they have to stand up against gale-force winds and driving rain. A round shape means that the wind and the rain blow around it and cause less damage.

At the top he found he was over-looking a small hollow. It wasn't a valley, just a depression in the top of the hill, protected from the winds and hidden from view. It had been cleared once, but was now covered in waist-high grass. In among the grass were graves. It was a cemetery.

Vincent pulled away the grass so that he could read the worn headstones. Two of the graves belonged to children of the lighthouse keepers. In the middle was a larger monument with an anchor carved on it above the grave of three sailors who

had lost their lives in the Refuge Bay
Disaster in 1852. It said it was erected by
Keeper Jackson and his family. The stone
was badly worn. Vincent could just make
out that 53 people had been lost in the
"disaster", the name of a ship was
mentioned but it was too worn to read.
Vincent wondered what had happened
during the Refuge Bay Disaster. How
had all those people died?

By the time he got back to the house,
he was exhausted. He built up the fire
and fell asleep in his armchair. He didn't
wake until Dad came home.

After dinner, Vincent was turning his
coin over in his hand. Perhaps Sandwich
Island had a more exciting history than
he thought. Maybe there had been pirates
or smugglers living here once.

"What's that?" asked his father.

Vincent handed him the coin.

"This is what I got dumped for. I found
it on the beach."

"It's gold," said Vincent's father. "Not
British. The writing is in Latin. I don't
know where it's from."

"I wonder how it got there?"

"Who knows how such a coin would

find its way to Sandwich Island?" Dad had an annoying habit of answering a question with another question.

"Do you think it's from a shipwreck?"

"There's a story behind it, that's for sure. A shipwreck is unlikely, but who knows?"

That was quite a long conversation for Vincent's dad.

Some children who live in isolated areas have to do schoolwork by mail. This is called studying by correspondence.

Vincent spent the next morning working on a boring history project. He was doing schoolwork by correspondence. He didn't like it. Vincent was amazed at how little time schoolwork took when there was nothing else to do. He'd finished the whole day's work before lunchtime.

It was a clear day when he set out, but, by the time he got to the lighthouse, it was raining. As he sat up with the lenses at the top of the lighthouse, a blanket of fog rolled in off the sea and surrounded the lighthouse. In less than five minutes, he could see nothing at all. The wind suddenly died and the fog hung around the lighthouse. It was an eerie feeling. He was worried that he might get lost if he went out into the fog. He'd just have to wait until it lifted. Bazza settled down. He was probably used to spending a lot

of time in the lighthouse. There was
nothing else to do. Vincent made himself
as comfortable as he could in the creaky
old chair and started reading the
lighthouse journals.

The first lighthouse keeper was called
Mr Baggot. He sounded like a grumpy
old man who couldn't bear to let his
assistant sit around with nothing to do.
When he wasn't tending the light, Mr
Baggot had him mending fences, painting
sheds and counting stores. It didn't
sound like a very exciting life.

Vincent was about to give up on the
journals when he came across a small
entry written in the margin in 1852. It
was after Mr Baggot had complained
about the assistant keeper asking if he
could whitewash his kitchen.

An unnecessary waste of supplies, wrote
the lighthouse keeper indignantly. Then
came the entry written in the margin. *Yes,
Billy Baggot, you know best, you old—*. It
must have been the assistant keeper.
Vincent smiled at the act of rebellion.

In the next entry, Mr Baggot had
written about the weather worsening.

A sudden storm, he wrote in his large

In the 1800s
lighthouses
used oil
lamps to
produce
light. The oil
used was
whale oil,
seal oil or
rape-seed
oil.
Lighthouse
keepers
spent much
of their time
making sure
that the
flame
burned
correctly.

loopy handwriting. *Thunder, lightning. The ocean one mighty mass of whirlwinds throwing the sea up a great height. A proper cyclone.*

The storm might have started suddenly but it had hung on for several days. It was the worst Mr Baggot had ever seen. The next day a sailing ship was sighted to the east of Lighthouse Point.

She is a three-masted barque of some 500 tons. Through the glass I can see that she has lost her main mast. She is signalling for assistance.

There was another brief entry the next day.

The sailing ship Christobel is wrecked.

The next entry was written by whoever wrote in the margin before. Vincent read the shaky writing and could imagine the shocked assistant keeper trying to steady his trembling pen.

The Christobel was blown onto rocks at the northern end of Refuge Bay. We got a line out to her using the rocket, but the surf was too severe. Three sailors tried to get ashore but all drowned. Mr Baggot was lost too, trying to

Rockets were sometimes used to help rescue survivors from wrecked ships. A rope was fastened to the rocket which was then fired at the wreck. If it reached the ship someone secured the rope to the wreck and used it to help them get to shore.

cyclone: *a violent tropical storm which blows in a circular motion.*

save them. It was the worst day I have ever
known. Of the 53 souls on board, only two
have survived. We will have a service to bury
the dead tomorrow.

The fog thinned and Vincent went
to the cemetery on his way back to
the house. He pulled up more grass
until he found Mr Baggot's grave. It was
a simple flat stone set into the ground.

In remembrance of William Henry Baggot
Sandwich Island lighthouse keeper 1846-1852
Drowned 5 September 1852 in the line of duty

Poor Mr Baggot, thought Vincent,
shivering in the damp, foggy air. He was
a grumpy old thing, but he was brave.

The next day Vincent went back to the
beach. According to the map of the island
in the lighthouse, the beach Vincent had
found was in Refuge Bay. The very rocks
where Vincent had been dumped were
where Mr Baggot drowned. The bay was
relatively calm, because it was on the
sheltered eastern side of the island. It was
hard to imagine how the weather could
have ever been wild enough to wreck a
ship here. On the other side of the island

To protect themselves from the cold, seals have a thick layer of blubber and soft fur, both of which were prized by hunters in the 19th century. Fur seals were driven to the brink of extinction.

the wind was strong enough to blow a ship onto the rocks just about any day of the week. But not in this bay.

Vincent wondered if the *Christobel* was still down there on the seabed. He tried to picture the stricken ship, its mast crashing over, its sails torn to shreds by the winds. He imagined the sound of the splintering wood as the ship crashed into the terrible rocks, the cries of the sailors. He wondered if there were passengers or if it was a cargo ship. What would a ship be doing out there in the middle of nowhere anyway?

Vincent's old urge to solve mysteries was stirred by learning about the wreck. How would you go about finding out about a ship that sank a hundred and fifty years ago? If he was back at home, he could go to a library. Here, the nearest library was across the sea.

Vincent decided to try the Internet. He logged on, typed "Christobel" into the search engine box and came up with 133 sites. He looked through the first twenty. There were eight sites about a country and western singer, several about a children's author, one about a baseball

pitcher who played for the Chicago
Giants, and a couple about a racing horse
called Mistress Christobel. He couldn't
find any about a ship. He tried narrowing
the search by typing "Christobel
+shipwreck". There was only one site. It
was a listing on a Tasmanian shipwreck
database. The entry was wrong. It said
that the *Christobel* sank off Seal Island.
There was an email address—someone
called David Sinclair from the Parks and
Wildlife Department in Hobart. Vincent
decided to email him.

There was nothing else he could do.

To: Mr Sinclair
From: Vincent Visbulis
Company: Parks and Wildlife Department, Hobart
Subject: Christobel
Cc:
Bcc:
X-attachments

Dear Mr Sinclair,
I am living on Sandwich Island. I was searching the Net looking
for some information about a ship called the Christobel.
It says on your database that the ship sank off Seal island. That's
wrong. It sank off Sandwich island.
Can you tell me where I could find out more information?

Yours truly,

Vincent S Visbulis

A barque is a sailing ship with three or more masts. The two front masts have square-rigged sails and the last mast has a triangular fore-and-aft sail. A fore-and-aft sail is one that runs in the same direction as the ship.

That was the end of his detective work. He continued to explore the island though, and he drew up his own map and gave places names. He called his beach, Deepwater Beach. The point where the *Christobel* had sunk he called Christobel Rocks. There was a nice grassy hill that he named Baggot's Heath after the lighthouse keeper. He found a pretty gully sheltered from the winds and full of ferns that he called Visbulis Gully. He spent a lot of time walking around the island. He got to know where the wallabies and possums fed (when they were bored with lettuce). He learned to recognise different sorts of ships from their shapes.

Vincent didn't like to admit it, but he was starting to get used to Sandwich Island.

chapter 4

Uninvited guest

THE SUPPLY HELICOPTER was due again. The Maritime Safety Authority who owned the lighthouse and sent them food supplies each month, rang to say there had been a delay and the helicopter wouldn't arrive until after lunch.

"I don't need to be here, Vincent," Dad said. "You can take care of everything."

There was nothing to take care of really. It was just a matter of helping the pilot unload and then starting in on the cake and biscuits that Mum sent. Vincent could handle that.

He remembered his excitement the first time the helicopter came. The first month had been the longest four weeks of his life. He was so pleased to see the helicopter he had jumped up and down like a three-year-old. At the end of each month, the food supplies were down to the tins of really boring stuff like beetroot and sardines, so he was looking forward to getting fresh food. There would be new videos and stuff from his mum as well. But it wasn't such a big deal as it had been the first time.

The helicopter appeared as a distant dot in the sky at 1.15 p.m. There hadn't been any rain for a few days and the ground was dry for once. As the helicopter landed, its rotors stirred up a cloud of dust. Vincent shut his eyes until the noise of the rotors stopped. When he opened them again, through the settling dust Vincent could see a figure getting out of the helicopter. It wasn't the pilot. It was a tall young woman wearing jeans and a purple jacket. She strode towards Vincent.

"Hi, you must be Vincent." She reached out and shook his hand.

Vincent just stood and stared at her. The pilot started unloading packages as if nothing unusual had happened.

"Who are you?" Vincent asked when he found his voice.

She pulled off a hair tie and released a

mass of dark curly hair. "I'm Merryn Randall. I'm going to do some under-water photography for your father. He probably forgot to tell you. That's just like Stan," she chuckled.

Stan? No-one ever called his father by his first name. Everyone respected Dr Stanislaus Visbulis, the famous wildlife photographer. People who knew him well called him Dr V. or Vis. Even his mother didn't call him Stan. Vincent didn't have time to ask questions, he had to help the pilot unload the diesel.

While he was doing that, Ms Randall was unloading a pile of other stuff. A big pile. Air tanks, a compressor and a large underwater camera. It looked like she was planning on staying for a while. She put her diving gear into one of the sheds and then started moving her bags into the house.

"I'll have this room if that's okay." She marched into one of the spare rooms before Vincent could answer. Bazza followed her around wagging his tail. It must have been years since he'd seen a girl. After Merryn had settled herself in, she went to the kitchen and put the kettle on.

An underwater camera can be used to take photos underwater because it is inside a special case that protects it from the water.

33

Little penguins usually lay two white eggs in the middle of July. The eggs take about 38 days to hatch.

"I'm here to photograph the baby penguins when they go for their first swim," she told him even though he hadn't asked. "That should be in about two weeks. I don't have to tell you, though. I suppose you know all about penguins."

"Not really."

Vincent had only been to Penguin Beach three times. It wasn't a beach really, there were too many rocks to call it a beach. And it smelt bad. Basically the penguins did the same things every day.

They waddled over to the edge of the rocks in the morning, jumped into the sea and then swam back in the evenings to feed the chicks. That was the gross bit. The adults coughed up the fish they'd already eaten and the chicks stuck their heads practically right into their parents' throats to get at it.

"You must be very proud of your father," Merryn continued. "It was one of his documentaries that inspired me to become an underwater photographer. The one about dolphins."

Vincent nodded. He'd been forced to

watch all of his father's documentaries.

"Stan told me in his letter about the shipwreck you're interested in, Vincent. What is it called...the *Annabel*?"

"*Christobel*."

"And you found a gold coin on the beach?"

"Yes." Vincent didn't want to tell this stranger all about his shipwreck.

"Can I see it?"

He was angry with his dad for inviting her onto their island. Angry that he'd blabbed about the *Christobel*. Vincent pulled the coin out of his pocket. He didn't want to give it to her. She took it out of his hand anyway.

"You found this on the beach?"

"Yep, among some rocks."

"Interesting."

"You know about coins?"

"No. But I know someone who does. I'll email him from here. Can I use your computer?"

"I'm not supposed to log on more than three times a day."

"I'm sure Stan won't mind."

Merryn logged on and sent an email describing Vincent's coin.

"Who are you sending it to?"

"A guy I went to uni with. He collects coins. Specialises in old Spanish coins."

"You think this is an old Spanish coin?"

"Maybe. Hey, there's an email for you with an attachment. I'll print it."

Vincent sat down and read the email. It was from the man at the Department of Parks and Wildlife.

Vincent printed out the articles. Merryn was reading them over his shoulder.

2:15 PM, Christobel   1
To: Vincent Visbulis
From: D Sinclair
Subject: Christobel
Cc:
Bcc:
X-attachments

Dear Mr Visbulis,
I'm afraid you are mistaken. Newspaper reports in the Argus and the Launceston Examiner both state that the Christobel sank off Seal Island. There are quotes from the two survivors. I have scanned the articles and attached them. This is all the information I am aware of with regard to the Christobel. The wreckage has never been located.
Yours sincerely,
D. Sinclair, Maritime Heritage Officer, Parks and Wildlife Service

Printed for Vincent Visbulis VV@waverider.net.au

"So you were wrong," she said.

She'd only been there half an hour and Vincent was already sick of her.

"No, he's wrong. The shipwreck is mentioned in the lighthouse journal. And there's a grave. Two graves. One for three sailors from the *Christobel* and one for the lighthouse keeper who died trying to save them."

"Interesting. I'd like to see them."

"Aren't you here to photograph penguins?"

"Not for a while."

Vincent led her along the path to the lighthouse.

"So what are you doing on Sandwich, Vincent? Shouldn't you be at school?"

"I do schoolwork by correspondence."

Vincent walked faster so that she couldn't ask him any more questions. He didn't like the way this girl had barged onto his island.

It felt strange having someone else in the lighthouse. Merryn admired the view, sat down in the wooden swivel chair and started looking through the lighthouse journals. Once she'd done that she wanted to see the graves and then she wanted to see the beach.

Lighthouses usually have thick stone or brick walls to help withstand the weather and the waves.

"There's nothing to see on the beach."

She wanted to go anyway. She'd only been there a couple of hours and she'd already invaded all his private places.

"Bit windy isn't it?" Merryn said tying back her wild hair.

Duh, yeah. It was the usual westerly gale.

When they dropped down onto Deepwater Beach the howling wind was just a memory.

"That's better," Merryn said cheerily.

"Show me where you found the coin."

He took her over to the rocks.

"There was another coin there as well I think, something round and shiny anyway."

"So you think the coin might have been from the *Christobel*?"

Vincent shrugged. "Maybe. There was a storm the night before I found it. I thought it might have been dredged up from the seabed."

"Was there anything else washed up?"

"I didn't have time to look, I was busy drowning."

> **barnacles:** *small animals that live in shells and attach themselves to rocks or the bottom of ships.*

"Let's check the high tide line."

Merryn marched up the beach and started searching through the seaweed that was drying out at the tide mark. She searched for about five minutes and found a twisted metal shape covered in barnacles.

"This looks promising."

It was a buckled circle with thick, cracked glass set in it. It had two screw fittings. She scratched away the barnacles revealing tarnished greeny-blue metal underneath.

"It's made of brass. I think it's a porthole."

By the time Dad came back from the penguins he'd remembered that Merryn was arriving.

"I expect you've made yourself at home," he said shaking Merryn's hand.

"You bet."

Over dinner Merryn chatted to Dad about his work. Dad was rapt. Vincent never asked him about his filming. Bazza lay with his head on Merryn's feet.

"Can I check my email, Stan?" Merryn asked when she finally ran out of questions about the penguins.

A porthole is a small round window in the side of a ship to let in light and air. It has a watertight metal and glass cover. The metal used is usually brass because it does not rust.

"Of course, Merryn." It didn't look like she had any limits to her time on-line, Vincent thought.

There was an email from Merryn's coin-collecting friend.

"Hey listen to this," she said to Vincent. "Your coin is Portuguese and it's from 1556."

"That makes it more than four hundred years old."

"And guess what?" She didn't wait for anyone to guess. "The guy in the dress with the ship in his hand is St Vincent!"

"St Vincent?"

"Yeah, patron saint of ships back then, according to my friend. Now, that's really spooky. You were meant to find this shipwreck, Vincent."

Vincent looked at his coin with new interest.

Merryn sent a couple of emails and logged off.

"The newspaper report said that the *Christobel* sank off another island," Merryn explained to Vincent's father. "But the journals that Vincent found make it clear that the *Christobel* sank here. The graves confirm it," she said, helping herself to a big slice of Mum's cake.

"I didn't know you were interested in shipwrecks, Merryn," said Dad.

"I've been looking for something different to do. There's a lot of interest in shipwrecks nowadays."

"What would you do, photograph wrecks?"

"No," Merryn waved her hand. "I'm getting tired of underwater photography. I really like the idea of searching for shipwrecks. Marine archaeology it's called."

"If what your friend says is correct, Vincent's coin was made 300 years before the *Christobel* was wrecked."

"I know. Weird isn't it?" said Merryn sitting up in her chair.

"And the newspapers said it sank in the wrong place."

"Just the sort of mystery I like," added Merryn.

"Some journalist must have made a mistake," said Vincent, wishing everybody wasn't so interested in his shipwreck.

"I have a theory that the newspaper was misled on purpose," said Merryn.

marine archaeology: *the study of underwater historical sites.*

41

"Why?"

"I don't know why, but the two survivors must have wanted to keep the wreck's location a secret."

"Perhaps the *Christobel* was carrying something valuable," said Vincent. "Maybe they wanted to come back and get it. Keep it all for themselves."

"It's possible."

"Do you think there's treasure there now, under the water somewhere?" Vincent asked.

"Not if the survivors' plan worked, it'd be long gone."

Vincent went to bed. He should have been pleased, but he wasn't. He'd wanted to do the detective work himself. To tell the truth he'd wanted to find out that it was a treasure ship laden with chests of gold coins. He hadn't been able to find out much at all.

In half a day Merryn had come along, found out all sorts of things and taken over his shipwreck. He looked at the coin and the figure of St Vincent. It certainly made it seem like it was connected to him in some way, that it was some sort of sign. But what did it mean?

chapter 5
Lost and found

"WE SHOULD GO diving," Merryn said over breakfast the next morning.

"What for?" asked Vincent.

"To look for the *Christobel*."

"I can't dive."

"You had diving lessons last year," his father said. "When I was filming at Phillip Island." He didn't mention that Vincent had hated every minute of it. The lessons were in a swimming pool and Vincent had never plucked up the courage to dive into the sea.

"I've forgotten what to do."

"I'll run through it all again with you."

"Vincent isn't an experienced diver like you," said Vincent's father. "He's already had a close call at the beach."

"I'm a qualified instructor, Stan.

Scuba stands for **s**elf-**c**ontained **u**nderwater, **b**reathing **a**pparatus.

As divers dive deeper, more nitrogen gas dissolves in their blood. This can cause effects similar to drinking alcohol.

I'll look after him and we'll only go out on very calm days. You could come too."

"Unfortunately I can't dive any more. Because of my heart."

"I guess that's why I'm here, huh?"

Vincent's father nodded. "It would be wonderful for Vincent to experience diving."

Vincent could feel that Merryn was winning him over.

"The water's freezing," Vincent broke in.

"I've got a wetsuit you can use," she replied.

"What about scuba equipment?"

"I've got a spare tank."

"Don't you have to prepare for your photography?"

"I've got a week or two before they take their first swim."

Vincent was cornered.

Scuba divers often wear buoyancy vests to help them float in an emergency.

He spent three days running through the fundamentals of diving. Three days listening to Merryn's non-stop chatter as she taught Vincent all the safety techniques and the hand signals. He read through a textbook and remembered all the bad things about diving. Drowning was the least of his worries. There was nitrogen narcosis, burst lungs, burst eardrums. He was going to die for sure.

They had to wait another three days before the weather was calm enough to go diving. Another three days of Merryn's chatter. She told Vincent her entire life story, even though he wasn't interested. How her father travelled a lot for his work. How she'd lived in lots of different places, four different countries, six different time zones. How she'd started a business degree in America, but dropped out because it was too boring. Then when her father's work had taken them to Italy she had done a diving course in the Mediterranean and started underwater photography. She'd been doing that for two years.

In the end Vincent was looking forward to diving so that he could have a break from Merryn's endless talking.

Finally the weather cleared and the sea was the calmest Vincent had ever seen. But as he stood on Deepwater Beach and looked out at the sea, he suddenly felt very scared. He'd had recurring nightmares about being washed off rocks by waves and he couldn't forget the

Divers learn hand signals so that they can communicate to other divers. The signal for 'OK' is made by raising your hand above your head and joining the thumb and the first finger.

terrible numbing coldness of the winter sea.

Divers use flippers to help them swim more powerfully underwater. The web design is similar to those of ducks and other aquatic birds and animals.

"This weather might not hold for long, Vincent." Merryn was impatient to get into the water. "Let's run through the pre-dive checks."

Vincent lifted his flippers clumsily as they walked backwards into the sea. He could understand why the penguins were so awkward on land. The air tank was heavy. Bazza woofed anxiously.

"I don't think it's a good idea either, Baz."

Then Vincent felt the water take the weight of the tank and suddenly he was swimming and breathing underwater. The sea was only about three metres deep around Christobel Rocks. With the surface just above him and the seabed just below him, he didn't feel too scared. Merryn had told him it was a natural reaction to breathe hard when you first started diving. He had to concentrate on breathing slowly so that he didn't use up too much air.

It was like another world underneath the water. The giant kelp, which looked messy and slimy when it was washed up on the beach, waved around gracefully underwater. There was smaller ribbony seaweed, pink and pale green, pinkish soft coral and striped fish. Merryn kept close to him, while Vincent paddled back and forth getting used to being a water creature.

He could see starfish, abalone shells and sea anemones wedged in crevices. It was so peaceful and calm, not scary at all. Swimming underwater was so easy compared with splashing around on the surface, fighting with the waves, so easy when you could breath air freely. He knew it wasn't always this peaceful. He reached out and touched the jagged rocks of the reef. He could just imagine the *Christobel* ploughing into the reef and smashing to pieces during a storm.

Vincent kept swimming, following Merryn. Then the reef ended, the seabed fell away steeply and suddenly there was ten metres of water beneath him. His breathing started to race as his mind told him it was dangerous, that he was about to fall into those depths and drown. He *was* falling. He'd stopped swimming and his weight belt was slowly dragging him

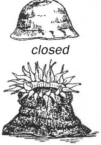

closed

open

One end of a sea anemone is attached to rocks or coral. The other end has a mouth surrounded by waving tentacles. Some sea anemones are beautifully coloured.

Humans float in the sea because they are less dense than water. This means one cup of human weighs less than one cup of water. Divers wear weight belts to help keep them underwater.

down. He slowed his breathing and paddled his legs to stop himself from sinking. Merryn swam up and he gave her the okay sign. She pointed down to the bottom, kicked out and headed down to the seabed. Vincent followed her.

All he could hear was the sound of his own breathing, which gradually became calmer. His ears started to hurt, but he didn't panic. He'd learnt what to do. He squeezed his nose through the mask and blew out until his ears popped. There were plenty of interesting things to examine: shells, rocks, crabs, but nothing that looked like it came from a shipwreck.

When they surfaced twenty-five minutes later Vincent was elated and disappointed all at the same time.

"That was fantastic," he said as he wriggled out of his wetsuit and dried himself. "But we didn't find anything."

"Finding wrecks isn't easy, Vincent," said Merryn. "Some wrecks take years to find."

"I thought it would be there, just past the rocks, sitting up on the bottom of the sea."

"It could be buried under sand. Or it

could have been smashed to pieces. There may only be fragments left."

Vincent couldn't hide his disappointment.

"We've got no equipment. No magnetometer to tell us if there's anything under the sand," Merryn said. She'd spent a couple of hours on the Internet and was suddenly an expert on marine archaeology. "Some people have spent years, decades looking for wrecks and had millions of dollars worth of equipment and still found nothing. We'll keep trying."

Baby penguins have soft downy brown feathers.

The baby penguins finally went for their first swim and Merryn had to be there in the mornings to photograph them. In the afternoons she was free to look for the *Christobel*. They tried day after day, but the weather wasn't going to hold forever. Merryn still searched, but after almost two weeks Vincent had more or less given up the idea of finding the *Christobel*.

He'd wanted to find a whole ship. Finding bits of squelchy wood that may or may not have been a part of the sailing

magnetometer: *a type of metal detector.*

49

ship just didn't seem that interesting. But Vincent looked forward to his daily visits to the underwater world. Every day he found another little corner of the reef to explore. He was getting to like scuba diving.

Bazza whimpered as they waded out.

"We'll be all right, Baz," Vincent told him. "We'll be back in less than an hour."

Vincent had decided to do his science project on marine life. He was trying to find out why some starfish had five arms and some had eight. He checked his gear carefully and then dived under the water. Each time he returned to the underwater world, he felt the same calm and peace as the first time. He couldn't imagine ever getting sick of it. As Merryn disappeared into the watery distance, Vincent was content to swim around the reef collecting up starfish to sketch when he got back to shore.

The marine creatures and seaweed had turned every little outcrop of rock into an underwater garden. Vincent carefully lifted several starfish off the rocks and popped them in the mesh bag he had tied around his waist. He swam over to look at a long, thin outcrop of coral growth

Starfish are part of the group of animals called Echino-dermata. This means spiny-skinned. They are unique animals because they have no heads or brains and they have five equal sides.

that was covered in waving seaweed. He looked closer and realised that it wasn't coral, it was too straight and too long. With his knife he prised off some of the little shellfish that clung to it. Underneath there was a metal ring. He could see now that the whole thing was made up of encrusted metal rings. It was a big heavy chain.

He followed its length along the seabed. It led to another shape encrusted with marine life. It was like magic, as he stared at the mass of marine growth, the shape suddenly became clear. This wasn't a piece of rock that the plants and animals had made into their home. It was an anchor—a huge anchor as tall as he was. If the anchor was on this end of the chain, perhaps remains of the ship would be on the other end. He quickly tied a marker to the anchor and then followed the length of the chain hand over hand until it disappeared over the edge of a sandy depression between two arms of the reef. Vincent couldn't see the bottom of the depression. His old fear of the sea suddenly came back. He didn't want to go down into the dark depths of the sand hole. He thought about going to

The type of anchor used on ships for many centuries became standard-ised in 1840 and is known as an Admiralty anchor.

51

get Merryn but he only had about fifteen minutes more air left. And anyway, he didn't want Merryn coming and taking over. He wanted this to be his find.

He switched on his torch. Its powerful beam encouraged him. It lit up seaweed puzzle shapes down in the hole. Hanging on to the anchor chain, he carefully swam down into the hole. It was another three or four metres to the bottom. He shone his torch beam onto the irregular shapes lying on the bottom of the hole, covered with waving seaweed and lumps of coral.

Just like with the anchor, as he stared at the encrusted shapes they took shape into something definitely man-made. It was a ship. Not a whole ship, just the bits that had survived years of sea and storms and marine life eating away at it. The ribs of

the hull stuck up out of the sand. A few decking planks were still in place. At one end was a tall shape. Vincent had been doing his own Internet research and had learned some things about ship construction. He thought that the tall shape must be the rudder post. Part of the bow of the ship was still intact, lumpy with marine growth. He had found the *Christobel.*

He scanned the bottom of the sand hole and in a few minutes found some broken pieces of pottery, a bent fork and a whole glass bottle with a rounded bottom. He took the two starfish out of his mesh bag and replaced them with his new finds.

He looked at his pressure gauge and realised with a jolt that he was almost out of air. With all the excitement, he'd been breathing faster. He was a lot deeper down than he had ever been before, he couldn't make out the surface of the water above. He started to swim up. His breathing was getting faster, using up his air. He knew he couldn't rush to the surface or he would risk getting decompression sickness. He tried to calm

Pressure gauges tell divers how much air they have left in their air tanks.

---

rudder: *a moveable flap which is used to steer a ship or boat.*

Scuba equipment was invented in 1943 by diver Jacques Cousteau so that he could stay underwater longer to explore the plant and animal life.

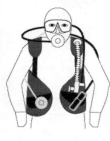

down. He had enough air. He just had to swim steadily to the surface.

He reached the top of the sand hole and an invisible force swept him up and slammed him into the reef. The force of the blow almost knocked his mask off. His eyes and nose were suddenly full of icy, stinging sea water. In his panic, he breathed water in through his nose. He instinctively opened his mouth and the mouthpiece floated out. He swallowed more water. He held his breath while he fumbled to find his mouthpiece. He couldn't see through the water in his mask.

Without the security of the regulator in his mouth and unable to see properly, he was aware of the power of the sea over him. He was an insignificant thing, a speck lost in the vast ocean. The sea had been waiting for him since he was a baby. It had got him at last. His lungs felt like they would burst. He closed his eyes.

He could feel the sea take hold of him. But instead of drawing him down to the depths, it was pulling him up and forcing something into his mouth. He opened his eyes, through the stinging blur he could see that it was Merryn who had taken hold of him, pushing her spare regulator into his mouth. She clamped his nose with her fingers and he finally sucked in a breath of air.

While his starved brain was flooding with oxygen and he was rejoicing that he still had the rest of his life to live, Merryn was hauling his body to the surface. She kicked him in the shin to tell him that he had to swim too. She pointed to her pressure gauge. They had very little air left. Vincent got his body working again and they swam to the surface.

The weather had turned. The sea was rough, the wind was blowing and it was pouring with rain. Vincent didn't feel like he had the energy to get back to the shore, but Merryn urged him on. Fortunately, the tide was coming in, so that, instead of sucking them out to sea, the waves dumped them on the beach.

Vincent caught his breath, and then pulled his finds out of the mesh bag. Miraculously the bottle was still in one piece.

"I think I found the *Christobel*." Merryn was angry. "Great, was it worth dying for?"

The regulator takes the air from the tank to the diver's mouth. It clips onto the top of the scuba tank.

"It wasn't my fault. When I came up out of the sand hole, I was picked up by a surge and smashed against the reef." He pointed to the rips in his wetsuit where watery blood was trickling out. "I panicked when my mask almost got knocked off."

Vincent shivered. He looked around. "Where's Bazza?"

The dog wasn't there waiting for them as he usually was.

"He must have gone back when it started to rain."

Hauling the tanks up the cliff was hard work. By the time they got back to the house, Vincent was exhausted. He revived the fire while Merryn put the kettle on. She was still angry.

"Thanks for saving my life," Vincent said, trying to get her out of her bad mood.

Merryn didn't say anything.

"I thought you'd be pleased about finding the wreck."

"I'll get around to being pleased when I've finished being scared and angry."

"I'm all right aren't I?"

"Only just. If I hadn't turned up when I did, you'd be dead and I'd be in gaol for negligence or something."

Divers spit into their masks and then rub the spit over the glass to stop the mask from fogging-up.

56

"Don't be such a party pooper."

Merryn smiled and brought Vincent a cup of coffee and sat down in front of the fire.

"So, you owe me, Vincent," Merryn said. "How about you tell me why you're here on Sandwich Island."

Vincent decided she had earned his confidence.

"I was making smoke bombs in the science laboratory with some friends."

"Doesn't sound so bad."

"The lab caught fire and burned down."

"Oh."

"It was this other kid's idea. I just went along because I didn't want to seem like a wimp."

"Was anybody hurt?"

"Albie lost a bit of his finger. I got expelled. Albie didn't. They felt sorry for him. The other kid was leaving school anyway."

"Not a bright thing to do."

"I know, but I've never done anything like that before. Mum decided I was about to become an arsonist."

Merryn nodded, "So she sent you here?"

---

arsonist: *someone who deliberately lights fires to cause damage.*

"Yeah. I think she thought I'd bond with Dad, or something."

"You don't get on with your father?"

"Not really. We don't have anything in common."

"Pity. He's a very talented man. You're lucky to have an interesting father like him."

Vincent took one sip of his coffee and suddenly sat bolt upright as if he'd burnt his tongue, even though by now it was cold.

"Bazza's not here!" Vincent was halfway out the door in his bare feet before Merryn could stop him.

"Where are you going?"

"To look for Bazza. He must be hurt or something."

"It's too late. You can't go blundering around in the dark."

"I have to."

"We'll have to wait till morning."

Merryn made dinner, even though it was Vincent's turn. Dad came home and the news of the wonderful find was overshadowed by the concern about the missing dog. Vincent couldn't eat. Dad tried to tell him that Bazza was probably all right, but Vincent knew that there was no way that he would voluntarily spend

the night outside when he could be by
the fire in his beanbag.

No-one felt like talking, not even
Merryn. Vincent went to bed. He couldn't
sleep either. There was a storm during the
night—the worst since they'd been on the
island. Vincent thought he was used to
wind, but this was different. It was
screeching and whining and seemed to be
blowing in different directions at the
same time. The shutters rattled and the
iron roof banged up and down. It was
easy to imagine the roof nails were
loosening, and the entire roof would soon
be ripped off.

chapter 6

Skull Cave

VINCENT WAS UP as soon as the sky started to get light. They were away by 6.30.

It was a cold, windy morning. Vincent thought of Bazza spending a freezing night outside, hoping that the old dog had managed to find some shelter from the terrible storm. But when they arrived at the beach there was no sign of him.

Deepwater Beach wasn't the usual calm place. The wind was blowing from the east, the sea was rough and the waves crashed onto the beach. The beach had been transformed by the storm. The sand dunes had been reshaped. Vincent had to find a new path down to the beach because the dune he usually slid down had completely blown away.

They called out, but the surf was making too much noise and the wind whipped their feeble voices away. Bazza wouldn't have been able to hear them even if he'd been sitting at their feet. They walked along the beach to Christobel Rocks.

"Do you think he would have climbed over the rocks?" Dad asked.

"I don't think so," said Vincent. "He never went anywhere unless he had to—except when there was food."

Vincent realised he was talking about Bazza in the past tense. The wind dropped briefly, at the same time as the few seconds of silence between waves. There was a sound. A bark. They all looked at each other.

"Did you hear that?"

"It came from the other side of the rocks."

Vincent started scrambling over the rocks, slipping and sliding, falling and bruising himself, forgetting all about his fear of falling from the rocks into the sea. Dad and Merryn followed him more cautiously. The rocks were covered with slippery seaweed. Vincent ended up on his hands and knees scrabbling over the rocks. Finally, he got to the other side and

found himself in another cove. Vincent looked around. There was a tiny pebbly beach, no more than ten metres long, before the rocks started again. Steep cliffs rose straight up from the beach. There was no sign of Bazza. Vincent could see that the high tide had washed right up to the base of the cliff. There was no way anyone, even if they had four feet, could climb it.

Vincent felt a sick feeling in his stomach. Then he heard a bark again. He couldn't work out where it was coming from. He scanned the cliff. It wasn't until he was about a metre away from it that he finally saw that what had looked like a dark patch of rock was actually a hole about two metres high. It was a cave. Just inside the cave sat Bazza.

"I've found him!" Vincent yelled.

Bazza didn't move, but woofed and wagged his tail. Vincent rushed up and hugged the old dog. He was wet through. From the tide marks it looked like the sea had come right up to him. He was lucky he hadn't drowned. Vincent examined him carefully. He had some cuts but he couldn't stand up. Dad and Merryn scrambled over the rocks to the pebbly beach.

Tides are caused by the gravitational pull of the moon and the sun on the ocean. The moon is closer to the earth than the sun and so has greater influence over the tides.

"There's something wrong with his back legs," Vincent told them. "I don't think they're broken. They just don't seem to work any more."

Dad was on his hands and knees examining Bazza.

"I think it's arthritis," he said. "The effort of climbing over all those rocks and the cold have just made his legs seize up."

"Why on earth did you want to come over here, you silly dog?" Merryn tickled Bazza under the chin.

Vincent looked around and saw something lying in the cave mouth. He picked it up, then dropped it quickly.

"Yuk. It's all slimy and it smells awful."

Dad turned it over with a stick. It was a dark brown strip, like a piece of leather.

"I think it's an ancient piece of salted beef."

The only torch they had was a tiny one on Dad's key ring. He shined it into the cave. They waited for their eyes to adjust to the darkness. Vincent tripped over something. It was a small box, broken open, full of salted beef strips.

Before refrigerators were invented ships could only carry food that would not go rotten. One of the main foods they carried was salted beef. The meat is preserved by covering it in salt for about five days and then boiling it.

arthritis: *a disease that results in sore and swollen joints.*

"I told you food was the only thing that would make Bazza do anything energetic. He must have smelt it from the other side of the rocks."

They looked around the cave. It was much bigger than it looked from outside and stretched back about six metres. It was stacked with boxes and crates. Vincent got down on his hands and knees for a closer look. He sucked in his breath and snatched the torch from Dad's hand.

"Look!" Vincent was almost speechless with excitement.

Dad and Merryn leant closer to see. There was something painted on the outside of the box. It was faded but there was still no doubt. It read "S.S. *Christobel*, not required on voyage."

"It's from the *Christobel*. All this stuff was salvaged from the wreck."

There was a woof from outside the cave.

"We have to get Bazza home," said Dad. "This can wait."

They went outside, blinking in the daylight.

---

salvage: *to rescue a ship or its cargo when it is wrecked or lost at sea.*

"Clever boy, Baz," said Merryn. "This is great. First the wreck and now salvaged cargo untouched for a century and a half!"

Getting Bazza back home was easier said than done. The dog couldn't walk and he was too heavy for one person to carry. Vincent remembered the rescue equipment he'd seen in the shed on Deepwater Beach, including an old canvas stretcher. He clambered over the rocks and broke down the door to get it. He didn't know where all this energy had come from.

They lay Bazza on the rickety stretcher and strapped him on. Then they took turns carrying him over the rocks and up to the house. Vincent watched his father and Merryn struggling to carry the stretcher, slipping and cutting themselves on the rocks, getting wet and bruised. Not everybody would have put themselves through this torture for an arthritic old dog.

When they finally made it back to the house, Vincent was exhausted. His arms and legs ached from the strain of carrying the dog, his knees and elbows were cut

The first inhabitants of the Bass Strait islands were pirates, sealers, escaped convicts and stranded seamen. The only Aboriginal people who lived on the islands were women kidnapped to be wives.

and bruised, but Bazza was in his beanbag by the fire. Vincent had no trouble sleeping that night.

The next morning Merryn had to go with Dad to the penguins. Vincent was keen to investigate the cave, but he didn't want to leave Bazza on his own. He sat with the old dog for a couple of hours and made sure he was comfortable before he made his way back to the newly discovered cove.

He took a gas lamp and, for the first time, he could see the extent of Bazza's find. The cave was packed with boxes and cases and piles of goods. Some of the cases were broken open and their contents spilled out. Others had clues to what was in them painted on the outside. It was mostly food and household goods.

Merryn arrived with some lunch and a Thermos filled with hot chocolate. She was very excited by the things they had found. Vincent was disappointed.

"It's all mouldy old food and boring stuff."

"It's all wonderful, Vincent."

"But where's the treasure? Why did they go to all the trouble of salvaging this stuff and stacking it in a cave?"

"This *was* treasure in 1852. White people had only been in Australia for sixty-odd years. This stuff would have been worth quite a lot."

"So why did they leave it here?"

Merryn couldn't answer him. Vincent sat down on a box of dried herrings.

"Don't look so disappointed. This is a big find. I bet there's nothing like it anywhere else."

"Big deal. There's just a pile of smelly old fish and some china ornaments. Where are the gold coins?"

Merryn put her hand on Vincent's shoulder.

"Perhaps your coin was the only one. It might have been a sailor's good luck charm or something."

"It wasn't very lucky." He knew there was more than one coin. He'd seen another in the sand.

"Even if there was a chest of gold coins here, we wouldn't be able to keep it."

Vincent turned to look at her. "What do you mean?"

"Shipwrecks in Australian waters are protected. Anything found on shipwrecks belongs to the government."

"That's not fair."

"It's the best way. Then the artefacts are put in museums where everyone can see them and where they are available for research. It's better than some private collector keeping them where no-one else can see them."

"Who'd want this stuff anyway?"

"I bet it's worth more than you think."

They spent the day making a list of the contents of the cave and taking photographs. Merryn wouldn't let Vincent open any of the undamaged boxes. She said they'd have to wait till the authorities decided what they would do with the find. But they could pretty much work out what was there.

There were seven trunks of shoes, fifteen boxes of dried figs, ten chests of tea, 200 bags of sugar, six cases of silk fabric, twelve cases of dried fish, seven crates of pickles, three crates of silk umbrellas, five crates of porcelain plates and ornaments, thirteen boxes of licorice and a number of boxes of dried beef.

"It still doesn't seem worth risking your life for," Vincent said.

In Australian waters, all shipwrecks that are 75 years old or more are protected. People may visit the wrecks but they are not permitted to take anything without a special permit.

artefact: *an item of historical interest made by humans.*

Merryn sat down on a crate and poured them both a cup of hot chocolate from her Thermos.

"You're right, you know. Whoever salvaged this stuff from the ship, went to a lot of trouble."

"They would have had to drag it across the rocks."

"Unless they brought it round in a boat. Maybe it was the lighthouse keeper, trying to make a a little bit of extra money on the side."

"The assistant keeper who took over after Mr Baggot was drowned? He wouldn't have turned smuggler."

"How can you be so sure?"

"I just know it."

Merryn was frowning over her chocolate. "And there's something else not quite right."

"What do you mean?"

"The tea, the porcelain, the shoes, the silk and the umbrellas were all part of the cargo. All imported from Hong Kong. But the food isn't part of the cargo, it's just salvaged from ship's stores."

"So?"

"The quantities aren't really enough to make a big profit."

Tea chests are wooden crates used to transport large amounts of tea. They are usually lined with foil to keep the tea fresh.

"Perhaps one of the survivors wanted to stay here and be a hermit. You know, do a Robinson Crusoe."

"You could be right, Vincent. But where did he live?"

"This cove is tiny. If he'd stayed here he would have been out of sight of casual visitors to the island or any passing ships."

"He'd need shelter from the weather."

"A cave would be perfect."

"There's not enough room in here."

They shone the torches into every corner of the cave just to make sure. There was no sign of anyone ever living there.

Alexander Selkirk, the real-life Robinson Crusoe, chose to be left stranded on an island because he was unhappy with the way he was treated by the ship's captain and he dreamt the ship would be wrecked.

They went out onto the pebbly beach again and searched every inch of the cliff. They walked up the beach three times before they saw it: another cave. There were two small entrances about a metre up the face of the cliff. They'd been hidden in the shadow of an overhanging rock. Vincent and Merryn had to crawl through one of the low entrances to get in. Inside, it was just high enough to stand up. They both flashed their torches around the cave.

Vincent's heart was pounding with excitement. Looking out at the sea through the two holes it was as if they were inside a giant skull. He closed his eyes and took three deep breaths, which was a mistake because the air was very musty. He spluttered and dropped his torch. When Vincent opened his eyes, Merryn's torch beam was swinging around the walls of the cave, bouncing off the rock surface. The cave looked empty. Vincent's torch was lying on the ground. Its beam splayed out on the floor of the cave. It lit up a small crate.

Pewter is a mixture of lead and tin and was often used to make mugs before the 20th century.

Vincent picked up his torch and had a closer look at the crate. On top of it was a tin plate, an old pewter mug and a book.

"Look!"

Merryn swung her torch around. Next to the makeshift table was a rough mattress. Merryn made a frightened little noise and grabbed hold of Vincent's arm. On the mattress was a body, or what was left of it. Just a bleached, white skeleton with worn salt-rotten shreds of clothing draped over it. Merryn was frozen to the spot staring at the empty eye sockets staring back at her. The skull had long locks of faded red hair lying alongside it.

The sound of the surf was magnified to a roar. It couldn't have been a very pleasant place to live. Vincent looked around the rest of the cave floor. He found a small wooden box with brass fasteners. He picked it up.

"Come on, Merryn. Let's get out of here." They climbed down through one of the holes in the skull cave and back out into the light.

chapter 7
The last chocolate biscuit

B AZZA WAS VERY PLEASED to see them. He even managed to get out of his beanbag to welcome them.

Vincent sat down by the fire with the box on his lap. Merryn was impatient to open it. Vincent was thinking about the skeleton they had found. These things belonged to him, a real person. He didn't want to rush it.

Vincent opened the box. There were three letters addressed to James Ross, a carved Chinese dragon, a tin whistle, a photograph, a certificate, and a creased sheet of paper. Merryn fetched the print-out of the newspaper article. One of the survivors from the *Christobel* was called James Ross. Vincent picked up the photograph. It was of a young man in old-fashioned clothes standing next to an older woman wearing a bonnet.

"I think that's who we found today," she said, pointing to the man.

"He looks young."

"He was. Twenty-one according to the newspaper article," Merryn said. "That's the same age as me."

"We don't know how long he lived in the cave."

"Not long I shouldn't think. He hadn't eaten much from the crates of food."

"The letters are from his mother in Scotland." Vincent read through the letters. The ink had faded and the writing was difficult to read. It was just news from home. Not very different from the news he got from his own mother.

The certificate said that James Ross had been working as a seaman on the *Christobel* for the voyage from Hong Kong to Melbourne. It also said he was born in Brechin in the County of Forfar in September 1831 and that he first went to sea at the age of fourteen.

"I wonder what happened to the other survivor?" Merryn asked.

"I don't know. There was no sign of him in the cave."

The sheet of paper had a hand-drawn map on one side and notes in a scrawly, unsteady hand on the other. They were notes about the location of the wreck of the *Christobel* with a rough map.

It took Vincent a few minutes to get his bearings on the map because it wasn't drawn with North at the top of the page, and the scale was all wrong. The *Christobel* was drawn right up on the reef. That made sense. James Ross wouldn't have had any scuba diving equipment. The food and cargo that he salvaged must have come off the wreck when she was still stranded on the reef.

Over time the sea and the wind must have broken her down until she eventually washed into the sea and settled in the sand hole where she was now. There was something else drawn on the other side of the reef round in the small bay which Vincent had decided to call Dead Man's Cove. James Ross wasn't much of an artist. It looked like a child's drawing of a rowing boat.

"What do you think this is supposed to be?" Merryn asked

"It must be the boat that James brought back from Hobart, anchored in the cove.

It is usual to draw a map with north at the top, and to include an arrow indicating north.

The scale on a map is a means of comparing the size of the map with the size of what the map is representing.

Merryn nodded. "I can't wait to tell your friend at the Department of Parks and Wildlife." She was very excited. "I bet he'll be interested now. They'll probably fly a diving team straight here. This is a real mystery: how did James die?"

"Could he have been murdered?"

"Well, yes, Vincent. Maybe. That's one of the things we'll find out."

Merryn's voice was rising with excitement. But Vincent couldn't see how answers to those sort of questions would come from the wreck itself.

"You think they'll let you help investigate the wreck?"

"You bet. I'm an expert diver. They'll be thrilled to have me on their team."

"You don't know anything about marine archaeology though."

"I'll learn." Merryn jumped up. "I've got some emailing to do."

Vincent didn't get annoyed with Merryn this time. He knew he was too young and inexperienced to be allowed to join the archaeological team. At least, if Merryn was involved he'd be able to find out all about what was happening.

Dad made a pumpkin pie for dinner.

Merryn opened a bottle of wine to celebrate that evening. Vincent was allowed to have half a glass.

"Here's to the *Christobel*," Merryn said, raising her glass. "And my new career in marine archaeology."

They clinked glasses. Merryn told them all about the famous wrecks she would investigate after the *Christobel*. Bazza finished off the pumpkin pie.

Marine archaeologists use special equipment to draw maps under water.

Dad had already gone to Penguin Beach when Vincent got up the next morning. Merryn was still asleep.

"Nice day, Bazza," Vincent said to the dog. "Warm enough for breakfast on the terrace, I reckon."

There wasn't a terrace, just a crumbly verandah, but it was sunny and warm out there. And the wind wasn't too bad. Vincent took his toast and tea outside and sat on a creaky bench.

He heard Merryn get up and go straight to the computer to check the email. She came out on to the verandah.

"What's wrong?" She looked miserable. This wasn't the cheerful bubbly Merryn he knew. She handed him a printout of an email.

4:15 PM +1100, Christobel   1
To: Vincent Visbulis
From: D Sinclair
Subject: Christobel
Cc:
Bcc:
X-attachments

Dear Ms Randall,
We will of course include the wreck of the Christobel on the list of
protected shipwrecks. Unfortunately the wreck does not justify
sending a team for an extensive archaeological investigation,
given the isolation of the location. Please leave the artefacts
where they are. We have informed the police of the discovery of a
human skeleton but they have said that in the circumstances no
immediate investigation is necessary. If any of the china artefacts
are of particular note we would display them in our museum.
David Sinclair, Maritime Heritage Officer,
Parks and Wildlife Service

> "There's more." Merryn handed him
> another email.

3:35 PM +1100, Marine Archaeology   1
To: Merryn Boyd
From: E McKenzie
Subject: Marine Archaeology
Cc:
Bcc:
X-attachments

Dear Ms Randall, Thank you for your enquiry about a grant to
study Marine Archaeology. Unfortunately there is no such grant, in
fact Marine Archaeology is not a course offered by this university.
Yours sincerely, Elaine McKenzie, Secretary to the Dean,
University of Tasmania

It was a week till the helicopter was due
back. Merryn was leaving then. She had
lost all interest in shipwrecks. She spent
most of her time with Dad and the
penguins. Vincent hadn't lost his interest
in the *Christobel*. Maybe no-one else
thought it was an important wreck, but to
him it was the most important shipwreck
in the world.

He didn't really mind that the
archaeologists didn't want to come and
investigate her. It meant that he had the
Christobel all to himself. There was only
one problem. Merryn was taking the
scuba gear back with her. He only had a
week. He begged her to go diving with
him in the afternoons.

"This is my last chance, Merryn," he
pleaded.

Fortunately the weather was good and
Vincent was able to go diving every day.
Merryn went down with him each
afternoon and paddled around Refuge
Bay. But her interest in shipwrecks had
disappeared as quickly as it had grown.

Vincent had read on the Internet about
mapping a shipwreck site. He didn't have
all the right equipment to mark it out, but
he did what he could with some iron

fence posts and string. Once he had some reference points he could measure distances and draw a plan of the wreck using a waterproof dive slate.

Over the week he managed to make up quite a nice drawing of the wreck from the rough sketches he did on the dive slate. He thought he would make a display of all of his finds in the lighthouse.

He was doing his history project on the wreck. Part of it was a presentation. His presentation would have to be on paper, but at least he could photograph his finds. He carried back some of the pieces of china, one of the silk umbrellas and some of the less smelly food items from the cave and arranged them on the desk with cards to describe what they were. He pinned up his drawing of the wreck site and photographs of the grave of the drowned sailors as well as a complete list of the salvaged cargo found in the cave.

He also displayed the porthole, the torpedo bottle, the bent fork and his coin. The shiny gold coin looked out of place among the other tarnished and broken pieces. Then Vincent scanned copies of

James Ross's letters and the other documents from his box and pinned them up as well. He left the originals in the box.

Vincent sat back with a cup of tea and the very last chocolate biscuit and surveyed his work. He was pleased with it. James Ross's box was on his lap. He wasn't sure whether to put that on display or not. It contained James's private things and Vincent felt that he should probably take it back to the cave where he found it.

He thought a lot about the dead sailor. Why had he come back to Sandwich after he'd been rescued? What was so special about this island that he was prepared to live in a miserable cave all by himself? He would never find out. He and Merryn and Dad were probably the only people in the world who knew James Ross died here. It would be a mystery forever.

Bazza hobbled over. His legs were fine again, but he put on a limp whenever he wanted something. He was hoping to get a piece of the chocolate biscuit. Vincent ignored him. Bazza nudged the box with his nose so that he could reach the biscuit.

When glass bottles were first made they had rounded bottoms not flat bottoms. They are called torpedo bottles. Often the brand name or pictures were moulded into the glass.

The box fell onto the floor. Something rolled out. Something bright and shiny. It was a coin, just like his. It had somehow been hidden in the box. Two coins, plus the other one he'd seen on the beach. Vincent looked at the map that James Ross had drawn, at the boat in the cove near Deepwater Beach. Perhaps it wasn't a drawing of James's boat. Perhaps James Ross had found another wreck.

"So you think there is another wreck?" his father asked that evening.

"I think there could be," Vincent said. "A much older wreck. Maybe even with some treasure on board."

"You haven't got much evidence."

"I know, but I have a feeling."

"A feeling?"

"I can't explain it. I'm just sure it's down there. And I'm sure James Ross found the wreck, and pretended the *Christobel* was wrecked somewhere else so that no-one else would find the treasure."

"Portuguese ships were exploring these seas three or four hundred years ago," said Vincent's father. "But I don't think they would have got as far as this."

"James Ross wouldn't have been able to go diving." Merryn said. "How could he have found a wreck?"

Vincent shrugged. He didn't feel like arguing with them.

"I think I'll have an early night."

He wasn't tired, he just wanted to think. He was working out a theory. James and the other survivor from the *Christobel* would have had to wait on the island for a ship to come and take them to the mainland. Vincent knew from the journals that the supply ship only came every six months. They might have had to wait for months. Lots of time to kill. What would they have done with their time? Same as he did. Get very bored and explore the island. Perhaps they found another wreck, a lot older than the *Christobel* and with a cargo of gold. Maybe they thought up a plan to come back and get the gold. He decided to keep his theories to himself. Dad and Merryn would say he was just dreaming.

Portuguese shipping records mention several ships that were sailing in the Southern Hemisphere in the 16th century. One ship, the *Santa Ysabel*, was searching for the Great Southland in 1595. It disappeared and was never seen again.

chapter 8
Wrecked hopes

VINCENT TRIED to get Merryn to go diving with him again so that he could investigate Dead Man's Cove, but she wouldn't. Two days later, the supply helicopter came and Merryn left. She was going to study the planets, which she'd suddenly become very interested in.

The weather was quite sunny. Vincent needed an easier way to get to the cove. He cut a path through the bush to the other side of the cove where the cliff wasn't so steep and he could scramble down. It wasn't easy, but it was better than crawling over the slippery rocks.

He had to look for the other wreck. He couldn't dive but at least he could snorkel. He carried the wetsuit and flippers down to the cove and swam out into Dead Man's Cove. He didn't really

know what he was looking for. The
Christobel was almost invisible and the
Portuguese wreck—if there was one—had
been there for another two or three
hundred years. The marine creatures and
the sea would have destroyed it all by
now. If any bits has survived, it would be
those parts buried in the sand and how
could he know where they were? Still he
had to look. He had to try.

The marine growth on this side of
Christobel Rocks looked pretty much the
same as it did on the other side. The cove
was quite shallow and he could easily see
the bottom as he skimmed along the
surface of the water. Snorkelling wasn't as
good as scuba diving, but it was better
than nothing. He stared at every shell-
encrusted shape in case there was some
mystery shape hidden underneath. Every
now and then he held his breath and
dived down to get a closer look.

He knew that a ship from three or four
hundred years ago would not have been
made entirely of wood. There would be
iron anchors, some metal fittings, maybe a
bell, but nothing that was going to jump
out at him from the seabed.

After an hour Vincent gave up. He knew that he was not going to find the Portuguese wreck. He still believed it was there somewhere, but he didn't have the experience or the equipment to find it. Instead he concentrated on collecting a few interesting shells and bits of coral for his marine life project.

A shipwreck was found on a Victorian beach in 1836. The dark deck timbers were thought to be made from mahogany or cedar. Over time all traces of the wreck have disappeared. It is known as the Mahogany Ship.

It was quiet in the evenings without Merryn. Dad was as quiet as usual without her to encourage him to talk about his work. Vincent thought he'd better make an effort to start a conversation.

"I went snorkelling around the other side of Christobel Rocks today," he said.

"Hoping for a last minute discovery?"

"I guess so," Vincent said, a bit embarrassed. "I didn't really expect to find anything, but I just thought I'd give it one last shot."

"I think the Portuguese wreck will stay a mystery forever, like the Mahogany Ship."

"I did find some nice shells," Vincent said getting up. "To take home as souvenirs."

He went over to the dresser and

collected up the items he'd found on the
seabed. There were quite a few, including
a group of shells and sand all stuck
together in a lump. He brought them
back to the table. Bazza was lying on the
rug. Vincent tripped over the dog and
dropped the things he was carrying. The
shells scattered on the floor. The lump of
concreted shells hit the edge of the table
and broke into two. There was something
inside it. Something shiny. Vincent picked
up the piece with the shiny object sticking
out of it, bent and twisted, but definitely
made of gold.

Sand and stones pressed together may become hard, like cement. Items in sunken ships often become concreted, as sand and shells settle on them over a long period.

"Look at this" Vincent said. "What do
you think it is?"

"It looks like a cross," his father said.
"A crucifix."

"There must be another wreck there!"

"Maybe you're right."

There *was* a Portuguese wreck there,
Vincent was sure of it. There might only
be a few of her planks buried under the
sand. Maybe a few brass objects. If he
was lucky, there would be a chest or two
of gold coins.

This time he wouldn't tell anyone else.
This would be *his* wreck. They might
even name it after him. The wreck had

waited for hundreds of years, it could
wait a bit longer. He'd have to save up
and buy his own scuba equipment and
learn more about marine archaeology.

Vincent thought a lot about his new
interest. The sea still scared him, but with
experience he'd learn to get over that. For
the first time in his life he felt like he'd
found something he was really interested
in. Something that he would stay
interested in for a while.

He had a hunch that there was more
gold down there. He knew that even if he
found treasure, he wouldn't be able to
keep it. Still, he liked the idea of
searching for it. In another month or two

he would be leaving the island and going home. He had to think of some way of getting back. He looked over at his father who was busily typing up his day's notes.

"Dad, don't you think you could make a good film about finding the *Christobel*?"

"A documentary?"

"Yes. Maybe I could learn how to film underwater. So I could help."

"I thought you couldn't wait to get away from Sandwich Island."

"I've changed my mind," said Vincent. "I want to come back and look for Vincent's Wreck."

His father thought for a moment. "You could be right."

Where to from here?

Where to from here?

If you are interested in shipwrecks, there
are a number of places where you can
find out more about them.

First of all look in your local library.
There are many books written about
shipwrecks in general and lots of whole
books about one particular wreck.

If you are on holiday down by the
beach, have a look to see if there is a local
museum. Just about every museum near
the sea contains some material from
shipwrecks, whether it's remains of the
ship or some items salvaged from it.
There might also be a lighthouse that you
can visit.

Some towns and cities have special
maritime museums that contain exhibits
only about ships and the sea. I visited the
Maritime Museum in Port Adelaide and
found it very interesting.

If you happen to be in Europe, you
might be lucky enough to visit the Mary
Rose Museum in Plymouth, England or
the Vasa Museum in Copenhagen,
Sweden. These wonderful museums have
the remains of two great warships which

have been raised out of the sea. They also contain a great many artefacts from the ships.

The other place you can find out lots about shipwrecks is on the Internet. I haven't had the chance to visit either of the museums I just mentioned, but I feel as if I have because they have terrific Web sites. They are virtual museums where you can see pictures of lots of the artefacts on display and learn all about them. If you don't have access to the Internet at home you should be able to use it at your local library or maybe at your school.

Here are the Web sites that I mentioned:

The Mary Rose.
http://www.maryrose.org/

The Vasa Museum.
http://www.vasamuseet.se/skeppet/theship.html

If you'd like to know more information about shipwrecks, read my companion volume in the Phenomena series, *Watery Graves*.

Carole's note

Carole's note

My interest in shipwrecks started when I was finding out about the sinking of the Antarctic supply ship *Nella Dan* for a documentary film. The film was never made, but I continued researching sunken ships. I discovered that every ship that sinks has its own special story.

Sandwich Island is a made-up island, but I read a lot to get to know what a Bass Strait island is like. To learn about life as a lighthouse keeper, I read some of the lighthouse journals from the Cape Otway and Gabo Island lighthouses. I really did find an entry where the lighthouse keeper complained about his assistant wanting to paint his kitchen. And I did find the cheeky comment written by the assistant in the margin.

After writing about Sandwich Island it is now like a real place in my mind. I can see the lighthouse, feel the wind and smell the sharp salty air. I hope you got to know and like the island too.